Meditations
for
Bird Lovers

Ruth C. Ikerman

The thrush family, the curious roadrunner, the tiny hummingbird, the nest of owlets, and the many other feathered visitors to lawn and garden become lessons in life as Mrs. Ikerman applies her gift of Christian insight to each one.

Every reader will feel spiritually lifted by the Scripture verses and the beautiful meditations and prayers which the author has chosen, for she believes that those who share the pleasure of bird-watching can learn a great deal about the care of the Heavenly Father for all his children.

To encourage those who have not yet discovered this delightful hobby, there are helpful suggestions in each of the twenty chapters which will make bird-watching the rewarding experience it can be.

Meditations
for
Bird Lovers

Meditations
for
Bird Lovers

Ruth C. Ikerman

Ⓐ ABINGDON PRESS
Nashville and New York

MEDITATIONS FOR BIRD LOVERS

Copyright © 1972 by Abingdon Press

ISBN 0-687-24081-6

Library of Congress Catalog Card Number: 71-186825

MANUFACTURED BY THE PARTHENON PRESS AT
NASHVILLE, TENNESSEE, UNITED STATES OF AMERICA

Dedicated
with love and appreciation
to
Dr. Caroline Mattingly Prendergast

But they that wait upon the Lord shall renew their strength; they shall mount up with wings as eagles; they shall run, and not be weary; and they shall walk, and not faint.—ISAIAH 40:31

Preface

This book is based upon the precious Bible promise that all those who wait upon the Lord shall be given the ability to "mount up with wings as eagles."

When we lift our hearts to God in prayer, we do not have to plod in weariness, and we do not need to faint. Instead we may receive fresh strength for each day's journey.

One of the best and easiest ways to find daily faith and courage is to watch the nearby birds. They may be feeding in a garden outside a beloved home, come to a paved city parking lot for crumbs, or stop at the window ledge of a sun parlor in a rest home for the aged.

The birds find their ways almost everywhere, so that all who learn to watch and love birds have a constant source of pleasure, ranging through all the changing years of a lifetime.

From the birds we can learn more of the care of the heavenly Father for all his children. May your own life find renewed blessings of spiritual strength for happy service as you read *Meditations for Bird Lovers.*

RUTH C. IKERMAN

Contents

1 Wake up to a Song

Yea, the sparrow hath found an house, and the swallow a nest for herself, where she may lay her young, even thine altars, O Lord of hosts, my King, and my God. PSALM 84:3

One of my earliest memories is of my mother coming into my room at home and saying, "It is time to wake up and hear the birdies sing." How often she used this simple phrase in trying to get her sleepy family out of bed, to the breakfast table, and off to school.

It was many years later before I glimpsed the profound truth inherent in her happy phrase. Blessed is the person who can wake up to a song—whether this means the song of the nearby birds, or one coming from a cheerful disposition. The birds sing their matins of praise, but those who love the birds often overlook this attitude of thankfulness for the new day.

All religions since antiquity have placed great value on meditation and prayer, often in the early morning hours. The point of such a time of silent communion surely is to enable the human heart to offer up its praises and thanks to God, much as do the birds in their early morning songs.

In the midst of personal problems begging for solution, or staggering sorrows, there is sustaining strength in remembering this habit of the birds. If the birds can sing at the break of day before beginning the task of hunting through the garden grass for the means of physical survival, then surely as a child of God, made in his image, I can approach the earning of my own daily bread with a song in my heart.

Wherever the duties or pleasures of life may take each of us in the changing years, the birds are there before us with their patterns of song. On a trip around the world by freighter, my husband and I watched the birds almost every day from the rolling deck. As the ship found its way across the waves from San Francisco to Yokohama, Japan, birds followed the ship each day, apparently resting on the waves during the night. Somehow they would catch up with the ship the next morning, when it was time for the galley remnants to be thrown overboard.

One such bird had an unusual wing span, probably because of an injury, and was always the last to arrive, with a great flapping motion. When we queried the captain, he said this bird had made many trips across the ocean with him, adding this delightful

comment: "If you were a bird would you have anything better to do than to follow this ship?"

Then there was a fat robin with red breast, looking
like a fugitive from a British greeting card of ancient vintage. He arrived at the windowsill of our
London hotel on a cold, foggy November day, giving
a cheerful chirp to indicate the weather was not
about to bother the traditional morning song.

Flashing wings of orange, blue, and crimson
against the lush green of the Guatemalan highlands
and the coffee *fincas,* the macaws have offered their
rare, enchanting beauty.

In an Australian garden of fragrant pink and blue
flowers, we watched the homeowner digging in the
moist freshly turned soil. A bright kookaburra
swooped down to take the insects and worms un-
earthed by his gardener friend.

When we visited the Holy Land it was a joy to
feed a tiny sparrow, which joined us near the suc-
culent bush of the familiar "hen and chicken" plant.

Wherever we may live, there is evidence that the
birds have truly made their home in God's world,
adding songs of joy and offering to share with all
who will take time to listen. Each day the birds ask
us to wake up to a song as we face our opportunities
for service and happiness.

Dear God, please forgive us for our failure to listen to the evidences of thy goodness to us. We take even the songs of the birds for granted, failing to listen to the harmonious calls surrounding us as we begin the new day's work. The discord of our own inner hearts is so loud that we cannot hear the harmony which is placed here for our joy. Grant us first the ability to listen, and then to absorb this melodic beauty into our hearts. From the song within may there come service without as expressed in our contacts with our friends day by day. Keep us from a sad, plodding sense of duty which destroys the true spirit of usefulness, and give us joyous songs of praise and thanksgiving for daily blessings. Amen.

Suggestions for Bird-watching Enjoyment:

Bird lovers often turn into "bird watchers," a delightful hobby for all ages. Yet some hesitate to begin, thinking this calls for special knowledge and equipment. Instead, true bird-watching calls for looking and listening in leisure, and may start at any time in life. Begin where you are today by looking out a window to see what birds are in your own neighborhood. A friend who felt sure she had no birds at all telephoned to report she had seen three very different birds in one afternoon from her kitchen window. She had taken the first step toward bird-watching enjoyment. Learning their names and songs would be a later pleasure.

2 Splashing in the Birdbath

The beast of the field shall honour me, the dragons and the owls: because I give waters in the wilderness, and rivers in the desert, to give drink to my people, my chosen. ISAIAH 43:20

A sure way to attract birds to any garden is to place a birdbath on the grass or near a shady tree. There is something about the freshness of a bowl of water which attracts many birds, not only for cool drinks, but for the fun of splashing with their wings.

First the birds will jump in with their tiny feet and then in what seems "deep-knee bending" will thoroughly immerse themselves in the water. Next, with a shaking motion, they manage to get more water into the soft fuzzy part of their wings, while brushing it off the tougher top feathers. Down again they go, this time putting the entire head under water for a second.

Sometimes they make a game of the act of bathing, staying on longer than we can spare time to watch from the big panoramic window looking down over the valley stretching below.

When the first small birds of the season arrive to be taught the daily act of cleanliness, the mothers first encourage the babies to splash and play. The bird mothers do not hurry the process, but let the baby birds splash to their hearts' content, while they keep a sharp lookout for predators. Finally they give an insistent call, apparently trying to get the young to move out of the water. Their "peep" in reply sounds as if they were begging like small children, "Oh, please, let us stay just a little while longer."

When the time comes that the young birds must learn how to bathe themselves, meticulous care is given to showing them just how to bend in the water, how long to stay, and how to use the tiny beak as a comb or preening instrument. Cleanliness matters to the bird families of the garden, and they sing as they bathe, happy for the clear cool water provided. Eagerly they return to the birdbath, day after day, following their ritual.

Watching this ceremony with us one day was a war veteran. His eyes never left the birds, but finally when he turned toward us, there was a faraway look in them. For the first time he talked of his war experience as he asked us bluntly, "Do you have any idea how wonderful water is?"

In his time of imprisonment, he had remembered

17

the blissful joy of taking a bath at home with water and soap. He had dreamed of standing under a shower and letting warm water relax his tired back. "Water is so wonderful, and we take it all for granted," he said as he turned back to the birds.

Surely the birds splashing in the birdbath remind us to enjoy the blessings of our daily routine. Recently when I was watering the garden with the hose in my hand, a bird darted down from the treetop and flew through the stream of water. In a few minutes the feathery creature was back, bringing another bird along for the quick dash through the suddenly discovered shower to cool the hot day.

Not afraid of the human standing at the other end of the hose, the birds enjoyed themselves, while I contented myself with watering the flower garden. There is no reason to feel hemmed in and defeated by problems when the outdoors beckons, with a chance to see birds and add water to the dry garden spots.

Life has its dry moments, too, and they can be changed into something colorful and lovely by seeing how the birds enjoy the water provided for them.

The Old Testament declares that the waters in the wilderness and the desert are provided by God, who cares for all his creatures and his children.

18

Father, help us to accept the water of life more fully, taking care to uncover life's dry spots, neglected through oversight or caused by sinful acts. We have the example of the birds showing that water is meant for cleanliness and enjoyment. We would be clean of heart, and enjoy our daily lives to the fullest. Forgive us the tensions which keep us from even looking at the birds, and help us to do better through a new awareness of thy goodness to all thy creatures. Take away our laziness that we may be alert to opportunities to serve thee by helping children in recreation, or showing them the marvels of thy outdoors. Put into our hearts the song of the birds as they accept what is provided for their care, for surely thou wilt protect us also and sustain us through the deep waters of life. Amen.

Suggestions for Bird-watching Enjoyment:

Attract more birds to your home by building a simple birdbath. The easiest to make is formed of just two items—a four- or five-foot pole placed in a hole in the ground, preferably anchored with cement to hold tightly in place. Then on top of this timber put a pan, such as an old wash basin or a dishpan, to hold water. More elaborate birdbaths can be purchased and easily installed. Ours is now twenty-five years old and is of cement molded in two parts, the upright standard and the movable bowl. We added a third part, a ceramic figurine of a squirrel, which we call Frisky. He presides over the splashing of the birds wherever the birdbath is placed in the garden.

3 Feeding the Thrush Family

> Behold the fowls of the air: for they sow not,
> neither do they reap, nor gather into barns;
> yet your heavenly Father feedeth them. Are
> ye not much better than they? MATTHEW
> 6:26

Until the walls of a home move outward
to include the birds at mealtime, much enjoyment is
missed. Feeding birds can add a new dimension of
happiness for all ages within the family circle. It is
so simple to plan bird "meals."

A tiny crumb left on the bread plate constitutes a
satisfying morsel for a bird to pick up in its beak;
but first that crumb must be thrown out to the lawn,
the sidewalk, or perhaps from a lunch bag on a city
parking lot.

It happens that my husband and I have sandwiches for lunch at the desk in our place of business,
and sometimes we are interrupted and do not finish
the bread and its fruit spread. Then when we return
home, we empty the lunch box and take the remains
of the sandwiches outside for the birds.

Several times a female thrush was waiting for

this treat. Mama Thrush would take the bread pieces as fast as she could pick them up, flying away swiftly from the lawn to the nearby trees. Then she would return and busily scratch on the lawn, searching for crumbs, much as a hen in a chicken yard.

We surmised correctly that she was taking the bits to a nest, but we did not know how valiant a mother she would prove in behalf of food for her young. One afternoon when we returned home with the sandwiches all consumed and failed to throw out a cracker or two, we heard a scratching sound against the glass wall on the porch.

Going over to the door to decipher the unexpected sound, we found Mama Thrush fluttering back and forth. It was plain to see she had conquered her fear of the house to come forward boldly and ask for food. So of course we gave her bread from the bread box, crumbling it in our hands as we walked toward the lawn.

She alone was the bird to come to the porch, asking for food if we failed to take it outside to her. Then one Sunday afternoon she returned with three fine chicks in tow. The baby birds seemed not the least bit afraid, but fluttered back and forth along the bricks on the porch like bouncing balls, imitating their proud mother. Obviously she had brought her family to say, "Thank you."

Seldom has any investment paid such large dividends as those which came from the shared crusts of stale sandwiches. The crumbs from the cake tray seemed to provide extra pleasure for the birds, much as a dessert after a good meal does for the family.

It was a happy moment when we decided to feed birds, and it has shown us how sharing even a little can add to the joys of living. This is not to say that only crumbs should be shared, but it is to point up the wisdom of making good use of everything which is available in the home.

Routing to institutions the magazines with which the family is finished is one way of sharing. There are pensioners to whom a book is a great luxury in the light of inflation.

Beads and discarded costume jewelry can have in their "retirement" from the wardrobe new places of service. When convalescents link them to the shiny lids of tin cans, unique wind chimes are created for the garden and the birds.

The sum total of the "little feedings" of life can come to a staggering amount of compassionate service when each family does a little. The time of the feeding of the birds at our home is a reminder to give thanks daily for blessings from God, and to try to remember to share from that which we have in order that others may be helped in meeting their own life problems.

> *Father, forgive us for forgetting to share out of our own abundance. We become blind to our blessings, always wanting more, and fail to give to others that which they can integrate into their own lives. Help us to know that the most we can ever give is a compassionate interest in their dreams and hopes, and the worst mistake we can make is to feel that all help must be of a material source. Grant us a vision of what true brotherhood on thy earth means—the recognition of the talents of others and what they can contribute to us, as well as our giving to those in need what they may want of our own personalities. Give us cheerfulness, courage, and faith in new measure that we may feel equal to solving the problems of this generation through wise sharing and understanding of equality and justice. Amen.*

Suggestions for Bird-watching Enjoyment:

Feeding stations for birds can be as simple as a silver foil plate, such as foods come in purchased at the delicatessen. Place this foil container in a limb of a tree, anchoring it steady by poking holes in two sides of the rim. Insert a yarn or cord through these holes and tie to the tree limb. From here it is easy to progress to the use of an old kitchen pan. Some vacation, a husband or son may want to build a feeder, for which many patterns are available in woodworking magazines. The simplest is similar to the birdbath—a timber in the ground, with a pan on top for accepting bird crumbs or seed.

4 On Golden Wings of Faith

> Where is God my maker, who giveth songs in the night; who teacheth us more than the beasts of the earth, and maketh us wiser than the fowls of heaven?   JOB 35:10-11

One of the most beautiful pieces of wedding music is Mendelssohn's "On Wings of Song," with its harmonious melody which seems to speak of dreams of happiness coming to rich fulfillment.

Often we long to be able to fly through life "on wings of song" as the birds seem to do with their songful flight. Watching a golden oriole swoop and dip over the pink roses in the garden, the bird seemed a beautiful picture of perpetual action.

Yet those who know birds best say that a moment of rest automatically accompanies the exhilarating flight, just as the human heart takes its rest between beats. The oriole's bright wings rest for just a moment before the next movement propelling the beautiful bird forward in the blue sky.

Natural elements hold the birds aloft in safety, even as they take time to rest from their normal motion of flight. With instinctive faith, the birds are able to pause to rest from action, and the flight continues undisturbed.

Ideally this would be the way for those who love birds to live their own lives—to the maximum of enjoyment and efficiency. If a proper balance of work and rest can be achieved there is great hope of accomplishment and pleasure in a life of service.

Too often, time is spent in a ceaseless expenditure of energy without sufficient time left to rest and restore the body's depleted resources. The secret which the birds share is that they can get their rest while in flight, continuing their serene way in perfect trust of natural laws.

If the human family is made "wiser than the fowls of heaven," then surely there is a way to learn a happy rhythm of living which restores energy in use, and keeps up a flow of strength so that projects can move forward successfully. The heart has its own golden wings of faith when it turns to God in prayer.

The mother who has learned to say a prayer for her children, even as she cleans house, is the one who has accomplished much in a spiritual way as well as a physical way. It is no accident that she feels less tired at the end of the busy day.

The father who has managed to use the time at a

stoplight to try to relax his tense fingers is better prepared to greet his children when he gets home than the father who has been gripping the wheel and gritting his teeth.

When at home there is virtue in taking a moment to listen to the birds singing from the telephone wire, or in a nearby bush. The bird itself may be in the temporary process of rest before resuming a long flight. As it rests it sings its song of praise to the Maker of the universe.

Prayer can become a means of lifting life upward on wings of song, for it offers rest from trials, surcease from pain, and is a constantly renewing source of energy for fresh projects. Such prayer needs to be accompanied by the beautiful melody of thankfulness, which seems to sound in the songs of the birds as they rest in the garden.

Inherent in each of us is the often unspoken wish to have our own golden wings of faith. We may not be able to fly away from routine, as do the birds, but we can cultivate their happy manner of flight. This involves momentary rest as the flight of the day moves forward, propelled by sincere prayer and trust.

Father, we are sorry we so often falter in our wish to make life easier for those who live with us. We become too weary of routine and neglect the periods of rest, so that our very voices become discordant with fatigue and querulous with criticism. Help us to learn how to balance work with rest, through wise appropriation of peaceful moments into our schedules. May we remember that when we are too busy to pray, we are too busy. When we cannot take time for music or song we are living life at less than its highest level. We believe that thou can place a song in our hearts in spite of whatever sorrows life may have brought, when we keep our trust and faith in thee and thy power. Humbly we ask now for the ability to move ever forward on happy wings of faith, toward the fulfillment of our dreams of peaceful living. Amen.

Suggestions for Bird-watching Enjoyment:

When the birds have been attracted to the garden through water and crumbs, and as soon as the bird

29

lover begins to look forward to bird-watching, the time has come to invest in an inexpensive bird book. We keep ours on the coffee table beside the large-print book of Psalms, which we use as a book of poetry in leisure moments. When a bird flies toward the big panoramic window, or stops for crumbs on the grass, we can pick up the bird book to compare its colored pictures with the feathers of the new arrival in the garden. The oftener both books are used, the more familiar the contents become, and the greater the possibilities for enriching life through words of faith and watching the birds in action.

5 The Curious Roadrunner

> But ask now the beasts, and they shall teach
> thee; and the fowls of the air, and they
> shall tell thee.   JOB 12:7

Glancing out the new kitchen's window on moving morning, my eyes saw a large bird staring intently at me. Not until the bird moved awkwardly down the driveway did I recognize my visitor as a curious roadrunner.

This was my first close encounter with this large bird of the Southwest. Sometimes he is sighted by tourists alongside a road, for he runs with his own unique gait, using his large tail for upward ballast against the wind.

Now as we stared at each other through the window, he craned his long neck forward, the better to see who was inside. Satisfied that I must indeed be the woman of the house, come to live on this hilltop, the roadrunner stuck out his feathered chin and moved determinedly toward the front door.

On tiptoe I walked to the door glass where I could watch him closely as he came onto the brick porch.

There he eyed me up and down from his firm stance. He inspected the new tile flowerpots at either side of the door, cocking his head as if to approve or disapprove the special "neon shaded" rose geraniums planted in the pots of colorful clay, souvenir of a trip to Mexico.

Then without so much as a backward glance, he turned onto the sidewalk, went sedately to the driveway, and walked to the large flower box at the top by the mailbox. There he paused for a moment, turning as if to wave good-bye to me, and went on down the road with as much dignity as a roadrunner can command.

He returned at evening to welcome my husband home from work. Glancing out the big panoramic window, I saw the curious roadrunner staring at the man in the chair. Quietly my husband put down his paper and turned around to stare back. They spent a few minutes thus getting acquainted with each other before the roadrunner took off across the narrow stretch of lawn, down into the sage brush hillside.

We learned that we could count on him to come back to satisfy his curiosity whenever we had daytime guests with their cars parked in the driveway. He had to inspect every new piece of equipment which came into the house, satisfying his curiosity like the proverbial town know-it-all.

Curiosity such as this has somehow taken on a bad name among human beings in modern society, where we live to ourselves and don't like nosy neighbors. Yet there is increasing evidence that alienation from one's fellow creatures is one sign of the current nervousness and mental disorders. It is difficult to draw the line between friendliness and abnormal curiosity.

A natural curiosity about the people we meet in life is sometimes construed as being too intent on the other fellow's business. Yet if curiosity can be accepted as friendliness there is opportunity for mutual growth. Care must always be taken to see that curiosity does not lead to prying into family secrets, or asking about morbid details of accident and sorrow.

Normal curiosity has its positive value, for indifference leads on to unhappiness. We are meant to be alive and interested in what happens to ourselves and others, and a healthy curiosity is an aid. Indeed, the first sign of recovery from depression often comes when the patient shows even a faint curiosity in someone beside himself and his own mental problems.

When well, we need to cultivate the happy "curious moment" in life, perhaps by going outside to look at the birds, even as the roadrunner came to meet us.

He adds to our daily enjoyment through his natural bird curiosity.

Once he has satisfied this curiosity, the roadrunner goes on about his own business, intent on new adventures. So our own friendly curiosity should lead us on to vigorous service and a happier future.

> *Dear God, please accept our thanks for the joys of curiosity, and the fact that there are so many fascinating things in life about which to be curious. Forgive us for allowing deadly indifference to come between us and new knowledge about thy wonderful world. We are grateful for the example of the birds which use their opportunities to look and to enjoy. Let us follow their lead in making the most of the beauty of the flowers, the colors of the sunset, and the patterns of the clouds. Take away from us the morbid curiosity which destroys, and grant us the friendly curiosity which helps and heals. Above all may we ever be curious about thee and accept even more of thy love for us as thy children. Amen.*

Suggestions for Bird-watching Enjoyment:

Curiosity as to the habits and manners of the birds grows automatically as soon as a few can be identified. As with so many other hobbies, the more you know about one bird, the more you want to learn about this bird and its garden mates. Soon the one inexpensive bird book will be well worn, and the paperback cover may be torn from being stuffed in the pocket to take along on a hike or picnic. It becomes fun to look for other bird books when shopping, and hardbacked volumes are available in all price ranges. Normal curiosity about the birds can be satisfied through study of new volumes containing pictures, approximate size of the birds, information about nesting habits, and climate preferences.

6 A Hummingbird in the Hand

In the Lord put I my trust; how say ye to my soul, Flee as a bird to your mountain?
PSALM 11:1

One who loves birds is in for some delightful surprises, but never had I expected to hold a hummingbird in my hand. These are the most vehement of birds, darting swiftly to the feeders to suck up the sweetened juice with their long beaks and tongues.

They hover like helicopters over the red flowers, and indeed this color seems to act like a magnet to them. With great swiftness they fly from one part of the garden to another Often there is a buzzing sound like a swarm of bees, and the tone seems to change if the mood of the bird is angry.

Sometimes two birds will engage in a friendly feud, each trying to keep the other from the feeder. Two who have lived for some time at our house fight so constantly that we call one of them "Pug" and the other one "Nacious." We have learned to tell them apart by their brilliant markings and peculiar manner of flight, each with a separate pattern.

Always the hummingbirds are a joy to watch with their swift antics. Sitting in my chair by the window one day at the hour of sunset, I noted out of the corner of my eye that the hummers were attacking the feeder with a vengeance, as though they were especially thirsty after a day of flight.

Suddenly there was a loud zoom at the glass windowpane. I jumped from the chair, dropping my needlework to the carpet as I turned abruptly toward the sound, thinking a bullet had hit the window. At least the glass did not appear shattered, but a streak marred the windowpane.

Outside I saw something iridescent in shades of red and black against the green of the lawn, and went quickly to the spot, for these are the colors of the neckband of a lovely species of hummer in our part of the world.

Lying on the grass, with its claws extended upward and the little head turned to one side, was the vigorous darting bird. It seemed impossible to think of this quickly moving bird as lying so still and immobile. I stooped to pick him up in my hands, and my fingers caressed the soft feathers.

Just as I got the tiny body into my hands, the bird revived. With a sound like a jet taking off on a round-the-world trip that hummer virtually exploded out of my cupped hand. He flew straight up and all but knocked the glasses from my face. I sat down on the steps and began to laugh at the incongruity of thinking I could actually hold a hummingbird within my fingers.

Who would dare have such temerity in dealing with such a graceful, powerful small figure of the sky? All he had needed was rest, and now he was returning to the feeder, where he sat for a long time drinking in the red liquid, as though his body needed extra refreshment after sustaining such a shock.

The darting hummer reminds vividly of the power of recovery in life. If we rest for awhile after sudden blows, we can often return to our own routine. We should be wise as the hummer in accepting extra refreshment, through food and fellowship with family and friends who want to help.

We may need to pause alone for spiritual refreshment in the quiet reading of some poetry about flowers, or turn again to the words of comfort in the Book of Psalms. We may be too tired or disturbed to turn the pages, but may just sit for awhile with the Bible in our hands, our hearts filled with memories, good or sad.

As God's children, we certainly have an inalienable right to rest after sustaining life's sudden hard blows.

And we have access to strength through prayer for comfort and wisdom as we return to our routine of service.

The hummer in my hand longed to be free to soar again with exquisite grace through his own arc of sky. After the needed rest he wasted no time in resuming his flight. Now his racing patterns charm all who watch as he uses his recovered vitality.

Dear God, let our spirits soar into the sky, even when our bodies are heavy with pain and grief. Show us how to recover from our mistakes and the accidents of destiny which would cripple our wings of hope. We accept now the strength which comes from believing in thy promises that we are indeed thy children. In a world grown smaller because of flight, help us to hold aloft beautiful ideals of peace through which the light of hope may shine with brilliance. While speed grows ever swifter, and the tempo of our lives is quickened, keep us mindful of dangers unless we keep a sharp lookout for temptations and barricades to progress. May we ever find our

*strength and serenity in thee as a constant
source for recovery and power. Amen.*

Suggestions for Bird-watching Enjoyment:

It takes a special type of feeder to attract hummingbirds, usually of plastic or glass with tiny holes into
which the long beaks can be inserted. Hummingbird
syrup can be made in as many different ways as there
are bird watchers. We use a ratio of three parts water
to one part sugar, adding a little honey for good
measure, as this is said to be needed for the fertility
of the birds and is a part of their natural food from
flowers. Always make the syrup red in color; no matter what proportions you use of water and sugar, be
sure to add artificial red coloring matter. Hummingbirds are drawn to red like a magnet, and repay the
syrup cook with their antics of swift grace.

7 A Finch in the Rain

By them shall the fowls of the heaven have their habitation, which sing among the branches. PSALM 104:12

The first sound to come into our house that rainy morning was the sweet song of a little finch, swinging on the green cedar hedge, now covered with silvery glistening drops of spring moisture.

Loudly the little bird sang up and down the scales, varying the pitch and the tempo in a glad refrain of happiness through the shower of raindrops.

Looking up from the morning paper with its gloomy front-page headlines of violence and financial concerns, my husband said, "I'm glad the little bird feels good this morning."

We had heard again from our yard the proof of the ancient proverb about happy birds which sing in the rain, knowing well the sunshine will come again. The birds seem to know that rain is an inevitable part of life's pattern, and they take their enjoyment in it as they sing ahead of the sunshine.

Yet the little finch had even encountered change

in its plumage through the rain. The brown feathers appeared almost black, they were so heavily covered with moisture. The cheerful red vest was a somber hue this morning, but the song which came from the bulging throat was unmistakably sweet.

The little bird had accepted its basic duller plumage of this day, keeping its intrinsic song of gladness, as though it possessed some mysterious inner serenity about the rhythm of life. Often bird lovers themselves find it difficult to accept the "rainy days" of life, forgetting the sunshine which lies ahead.

We speak of "saving for a rainy day" with all the financial burdens this implies. Only recently have travel agencies urged "Save for a Sunny Day," and this attitude has produced some exciting trips for those who have tried the positive approach.

Truly the rainy days pass, as the birds know, and their dark plumage becomes bright again as the moisture leaves their feathers. The winds of the season sweep over the little bodies, bringing a restful warming touch of healing. Soon the sun is out again, and the coloring is restored to full beauty.

Such a natural process takes time even with the family of birds. The songs continue, however, and this is not always true for those who feed the birds. Instead of singing while waiting for the sun, human families often complain about the burden which has produced the symbolic "rainy day."

Complaints have a mournful sound about them, whether they concern a financial problem, ill health of a family member, worry over a child's school progress, or dismay at the weakness of an aging member of the family. The situation itself is not changed by the complaints, but rather the problem is worsened.

One helpful approach is to follow the example of the birds who keep on singing when the outer circumstances are damp and cold. They keep alive the warmth of their songs, passed along from one bird generation to another, an innate quality of beauty which seems inherent in their creation.

Thus the Creator must verily be aligned with beauty and harmony also. Learning this fact can be one means of a more rapid recovery from illness or depression. Surely physical or mental healing will come in due time if the heart manages its songs of cheerfulness even though the outer problem has not yet changed through some better solution.

Glad is the song of the birds in the rain, lovely is the dark-colored bird in the storm. It goes in search of daily bread in spite of the rain, knowing that the returning warmth of the sun will heal and return the colors to brilliance, even as the song remains.

Father, forgive us our dark moods of depression and discouragement. Help us to know that we still have tongues to praise thee for past blessings, thank thee for the present, and to express to thee our longings and dreams for a better future. We need to be forgiven also for the way in which we have let our own black moods hurt and harm those who are closest to us. They have their burdens, too, and we only make them worse by a recital of our woes. Grant us the simple wisdom of the birds, and let us keep the cheerful tunes alive through the storms so that others may not suffer from the dimness of our souls. Guide us through the storms of personal distress that we may be strengthened for fresh service in the sunlit days as they return with fresh beauty. Amen.

Suggestions for Bird-watching Enjoyment:

Each bird has its own special song, as bird watchers learn when they realize that listening is such an important part of the identifying process. One reason some bird lovers hesitate to become watchers is that the sounds of the birds when written down in prosaic letters of the alphabet look like a strange foreign language. Often f, s, t, or v, c, h appear to startle the eye as someone has tried hard to capture on paper the exquisite sound of a bird. Another way to go at the listening is to try to hum the sound, or if you are a whistler, fake a rough imitation of the bird call. Records are available of bird sounds, and listening sometimes leads to starting such a collection, available also at seasons when the birds are away on their migratory flights.

8 Foster Mother for Baby Birds

I know all the fowls of the mountains: and
the wild beasts of the field are mine.
PSALM 50:11

One of the intriguing mysteries of bird
life is the way certain birds refuse to rear their young,
but count on other birds to become foster parents.
Notably the cowbird seeks out the nests of other
birds, often the towhee, to place an egg in the nest.
It then scurries on to another nest to place an egg
there.

Then the female cowbird is free to go on her own
selfish way, with no thought of concern for the eggs
and the possible welfare of any birds which may
hatch out into the wide wonderful world with its
tempting sky.

This process has brought the term "parasitic
birds," and pictures in some books show as many as
five layers of nests erected over such parasitic eggs.
Sometimes the mother in the new nest refuses to

accept the egg which is not her own. She just builds a new nest for herself.

In other instances the mother bird prefers to hatch out her own clutch of eggs and includes the parasitic egg. If this extra egg hatches out at approximately the same time as her own, it is interesting to watch the care she gives all the birds simultaneously and apparently without prejudice.

When the small feathery balls of fluff are able to make their way to a bird feeder, she takes turns in feeding each small "toddler"—her own and the adopted bird. Sometimes the feathers of her own will be a light brown, and those of the other bird a deeper shade, soon to turn to the black which features the male cowbird.

Fortunately, in their early days most baby birds resemble one another in the brownness of their feathers or fluffy fuzz, extending out over the brown nest much as an extra lining or a soft frill of embroidery in a bassinette. This protecting coloring apparently has been devised by their Creator to enable the maximum number of them to grow up to become the new generation.

Foster bird families are interesting to watch, for the young birds play together seemingly with no awareness of differences. Perhaps this is due in part to the way the mother feeds them in rotation. She will move first to one opened mouth, then to the second, and finally the third, perhaps reversing the order on the next round of food.

Without the help of foster bird mothers, some species would have died out long before this. The sleek black of the cowbird contrasting with the golden brown of its hood would be lost from the garden's beauty. Their usefulness in following the herds and disposing of parasitic insects would also be lost to the world of ecology.

So it is that without the help of human foster parents in the modern world the talents of many young people would be lost. Becoming a foster parent is a real challenge, calling for definite decisions to share family income and time with children who need such help.

Smiles of love await the families which become foster parents, whether to a small child or to an older one who has spent formative years in an orphanage. It is possible also to "adopt by mail," supporting an orphan in such a place as Hong Kong. Letters bridge the physical gap, and pictures of smiling children bring pleasure.

So long as we live in this natural world of both selfishness and sorrow, love and gladness, there will be need for sharing nests and homes. The foster parents in the bird world learn to accommodate to save the species. Serving as human foster parents brings much joy into many homes which love both children and birds.

Dear God, any of us can do more than we are doing now to help thy needy children, but we often hesitate because of selfish desires, and fear of financial failure or bearing burdens of responsibility. Keep before us the joys of sharing, even as the bird families are led to find their food for even the little birds abandoned by those who are termed bird parasites. Let none of us be tempted to move from our own responsibilities. Give us grace to assume more, lending ourselves to the solving of today's problems of hunger and need. Accept our thanks for all which comes into our homes from thee, and give us hearts eager to share with those closest to us. May we always be glad to extend the perimeter of our love to the largest possible circle of concern. Amen.

49

Suggestions for Bird-watching Enjoyment:

Birds have big appetites in spite of their comparatively small sizes, and never is this more evident than at the time when the mothers are feeding the baby birds. They make endless trips to the feeder to get seed to take to the nest. Then when the babies are large enough to come up to the feeders, it takes a long time for the mother to get enough food stuffed down the open beak of each fuzzy young bird. We have learned to buy bird seed in 100-pound sacks. This calls for a means of storing it, and we use a metal 20-gallon garbage pail, as this discourages rodents from getting into the food. Buying in quantity is also easier on the budget of the bird watcher.

9 The Big Battered Bird

Consider the ravens: for they neither sow
nor reap; which neither have storehouse nor
barn; and God feedeth them: how much
more are ye better than the fowls? LUKE
12:24

Where he came from we never knew,
the big battered bird which dropped out of the sky
and lingered around our birdbath until he was well
enough to fly on to some unspecified destination.

It was a shocking surprise to discover a bird of
such size sitting in the water, its bloody head cocked
to one side, a picture of complete weariness and utter
dejection, too tired seemingly to move until we took a
few steps forward.

Then with great deliberation, the bird managed to
raise a wing and with feeble flaps move a few feet
away to a point beneath the protecting hedge. It
made no effort to fly up to the nearest limb, but
huddled on the ground, as if to say, "Let the dogs
and cats come. I've gone as far as my strength will
take me now."

Even though we realized this big bird was a foe of
the little ones which usually frequent our birdbath, we

could not muster up the will to chase the stranger away in this condition. Because of the inherent fear of wild life for humans, it seemed impossible to try to help, except to leave the bird to help itself. We trusted in the healing power of rest and water, as sun and moon, day and night, moved around its quiet existence.

All the first day the bird rested completely, and at evening the smaller birds came back. Something seemed to tell them that the giant bird was in no way capable of hurting them at this stage of its life.

The second day the big battered bird managed to get to the silver foil pan of water we had placed near-by under the hedge. It drank and drank and drank, but refused even the tiny pieces of bird seed scattered nearby.

Not until the third morning did the bird sample any of the seed placed out as food. That was the day we noted later some evidence of its trying to restore the rumpled feathers to a semblance of order. With the large beak, it would peck away at some of the dirt and caked blood, until little by little the neck area began to show the blackish green plumage.

How good it was to watch the beautiful bird trying gamely to restore itself to circulation. Before the week was out we watched the battered bird take to unsteady flight, and move away from its place of resting near our window. Our last sight glimpsed the bird reaching the lowest branch of a tall tree.

Often do we think of the big battered bird, especially when we see someone with great ability who is bruised by sorrow or broken by temptation. There is a phrase current which says "the bigger they are, the harder they fall," which points up the need for constant vigilance. Indeed, a big bird is an easier target for marksmen than the smaller ones.

It takes great discipline and skill to keep life free from impediments. True bigness has the power to pick itself up again, dust off the pieces, and start over from there. This may mean a constant bout with alcoholism, real pain in withdrawing from drugs. Or it may simply mean trying each day to cultivate a more cheerful attitude to counteract moods of depression.

Even as the big battered bird withdrew, there is something inherent in each of us to want to retreat in solitude and hide away with our wounds. Often we refuse help from those nearest and dearest, and completely overlook the extra help which God supplies when we ask in time of need.

Sooner or later, we must return to our routine, even if scars remain. This restoration can be accomplished through contacting the love of God by prayer for strength while making good use of the available human resources for rest. Little by little energy returns for resuming the normal pattern of happy living.

> *God, it is so easy to slip from grace, and to fall harder than we expected at our time of temptation. Give us honest hearts to look fearlessly at our failures to live up to our dreams and desires. When hurt by those we love, or some of the falling timber of decaying institutions, let us cling to the inner belief in our own worthiness as children of thine. Show us how to find our rest in thee that we may never be homeless, but always have a place of restoration. Help us to use all our resources of friendship, love, and affection, when we need them. May we remember also to share these good gifts with others when they are battered and bruised from the burdens of the day. Keep us in thy loving care this day and always. Amen.*

Suggestions for Bird-watching Enjoyment:

Birds which are ill or injured automatically seek a place of rest away from the sun. Even in health, the birds like shade, since their food will keep fresh longer and the water will be cooler. If you have no regular shade from a tree, a makeshift can be provided by the use of branches from a hedge, or flower leaves and stems placed over two crossed poles above a feeder. Naturally these have to be replaced occasionally when the leaves wither, but they make a good temporary substitute. In the Southwest the everfaithful palm fronds make fine bird umbrellas, and every section of the country has its own sturdy, dependable foliage.

10   The Towhee Brothers

As a bird that wandereth from her nest,
so is a man that wandereth from his place.
PROVERBS 27:8

When a friend first saw the handsome
towhee of the Western sage which had come to our
feeder for food, she said, "But where are his friends?"
Often the towhee is a solitary bird, shyly spending
much time alone, and often leaving when other birds
arrive.

This beautiful bird has an orange breast, and at
first glance seems much like a robin. The jet black
head blends into a "man's jacket" of a lighter shade
of black, flecked with white.

As the bird swishes its tail and wings to wander
on further along its solitary way, there is a snow
white stripe to be seen, as chic as a neatly folded
white handkerchief in the breast pocket of a smart
dark suit.

With such handsome raiment it would seem that
this naturally attractive bird would be welcome in
any feathery society. Yet the towhee is such a solitary

bird that it was an eventful day at our house when this wild pet acquired a brother towhee for companionship.

Now the towhee brothers give us endless delight in their appearances at our bird feeder, when they return from their mysterious wanderings away. Silently they come back, and we glance out the window some morning we see the two beautiful male birds, returning for their food.

Larger now than when they first formed their association three years ago, apparently they have each set up nests in the nearby chaparral. Two females come later in the day for food, sometimes together, but more usually alone in their search, often taking food back to the young in the nests.

The two bright-plumaged male towhee brothers have set up their feeding patterns alike. They come at the identical time each morning, returning in the shadows of evening when most of the other birds are gone. In the late twilight it is possible to see their orange breasts, as the lingering light of the golden sun adds a special sheen to their native color. Sometimes there seem to be bits of gold glancing off the darkened hoods.

Never very close together, but always putting in a twin appearance, these birds are most welcome and prove of great interest to friends who watch their association. The towhee brothers will look over the grain and pick happily at the ground, walking around in circles but never quite touching each other's domain. They seem contented to browse in this companionship, making the green landscape more attractive to those who watch.

In their acceptance of each other, with a nice distance kept intact for their solitary nature, the towhees give an example of brotherliness to all who love birds. Finding a brother implies the willingness to grant to others met along life's wandering pathway a degree of solitary independence also.

Smothering in too much togetherness is a sure way to throttle the growth of friendship, and always adds problems to modern marriage. Giving children a chance to sit apart and think out their own imaginative games is one way to nourish their personalities before they enter the business world of machines.

We are each meant to have our solitary moments for creative thinking and deciding in what way to best use our talents and time. Thus we learn our true place in life and remain ourselves wherever we may wander in meeting life's opportunities and duties.

Only then are we ready to make our best contribution to those we meet day by day, as we recognize our common brotherhood. We can reach out our hands to others and double our pleasure in living as typified by the towhee brothers.

> *Dear God, we remember that thy son Jesus said that he himself had no place to lay his head, as he wandered with his disciples. He pointed out how the birds have their nests, and we observe that some of them lead their solitary lives from this point of habitation. For each of us there are the solitary moments of the soul, when it seems that nobody can reach us and that nothing can heal or help our distress. Be with us in all such situations, that we may know we are not alone ever so long as we turn to thee, Maker of the universe and of earthly children. Grant us the ability to love and forgive, so that our hearts may find release from solitary prisons and join in the fellowship of human causes. Amen.*

Suggestions for Bird-watching Enjoyment:

When bird lovers first begin to watch birds, the tendency is to think that all birds will act alike.

Nothing could be further from the truth. Each bird has its own special pattern for feeding, and its own nature, which may be shy and retiring or most aggressive. Part of the joy of watching comes through learning the idiosyncracies of the various birds, and seeing how differently they approach such an elemental matter as feeding. Each bird family will stake out its own feeding ground. Sometimes it will share with others, and sometimes it will not tolerate even one other bird within its range. If several areas can be provided for feeding, the joys of watching can be multiplied, as different birds go to the most compatible feeding station.

11 The Mourning Dove

Like a crane or a swallow, so did I chatter:
I did mourn as a dove: mine eyes fail with
looking upward: O Lord I am oppressed;
undertake for me. ISAIAH 38:14

It sounded like someone crying in the
treetops, but we knew it must be the mourning dove.
Soon a pair of the beautiful gray birds, with blue and
pink iridescent neck feathers looking like a rare
jeweled necklace, appeared near the feeder.

These birds instantly became our friends, making
our home their home as the seasons changed. Then
one day I heard the plop of a gun and came outside
to find one of the birds gasping on our lawn. With a
final call it was gone before I could get to its side.

Nearby the mate fluttered its wings in dismay, half
afraid to come near because of me, and probably
also recalling the frightening sound of the gun so
recently fired. Eventually love of mate won out over
fear, and it was a distressing thing to see the bird
return to the side of the mate with whom it had
browsed our hilltop daily in search of food.

How my husband and I had loved seeing this

beautiful pair of doves strolling together on top of the ledge near the cedars and then taking off in unison to fly against the sunset sky. Now there was only one, and it seemed to fly away in panic. Sadly we buried the mate. No longer would the firm wings let the air uplift so the keen eyes could look into the blue horizon.

We hardly expected to see the survivor again. Then one morning we glanced up to see the dove with eyes pointing downward, looking for seed beneath the feeder, alone among the smaller birds. Instantly my husband was on his feet to go outside to give the bird a special handful of grain.

It flew away and watched from a wire in the distance, and then returned. With real hunger, almost greedily, the bird began to eat the food provided, as though it had been away on a fast of sorrow.

The other birds seemed to sense that something was amiss and left the large dove to enjoy the domain in solitude until the meal was finished. Thus began a ritual which has lasted for over two springtimes. Still the bird is alone, confirming the tradition that such doves mate for life.

For long hours, the bird will sit on a tall post, just looking over the landscape, much as many older people do who have been bereaved of a mate. They may sit in a rocker on a home porch, or silently contemplate the world from a window in a convalescent home.

Somehow the sad sigh of the mourning dove expresses how many feel as their hearts come up against the sorrows of a world of war prisoners, financial problems, and loss of loved ones through accidents and terminal disease. The mournful sound of the dove reverberates through the hearts of many people.

Yet there is another way to spell the word by which they are identified, as a little boy recently reminded me. He asked, "Do you mean it is a morning dove, because it sings early in the morning after the dark is gone?"

Wise beyond his years, he expressed what the heart seeking comfort must find out for itself. The time comes when the word "mourning" must be replaced by "morning," with its fresh opportunities for service.

Something wonderful happens when we eventually realize that mourning can be turned into eternal morning, if we have faith and trust God, who knows the end from the beginning. Thus the mourning sound of the dove becomes a part of the song of life— the undertone to make us appreciate the harmonious blessings of companionship and enjoy each new morning of our lives.

Father, all of us have our times of mourning when it seems we can never face the morning of another day. We thank thee for the example of thy son Jesus, who accepted trials and sorrows until death, asking only to do the will of his heavenly Father. Give us this humility of heart, and a special portion of patience to be expressed in fresh hope and stronger faith. When we can no longer take large steps, help us to start again with the small ones, until we become strong enough to face life under conditions altered by sorrow. Let our mourning be turned into praise and ever greater trust in thee, our all-wise Creator. Amen.

Suggestions for Bird-watching Enjoyment:

One of the easiest sounds to recognize in the bird world is the call of the mourning dove. It is louder and more prolonged, and does not vary so much in sound and speed as do many others. Therefore this is a good place to start tape-recording the sounds of birds. Great patience is required, for sometimes a bird cannot be coaxed to sing at the time when the tape recorder is in place. If a songfest is in session, it is necessary to go outdoors warily lest the birds be frightened away. Often such a bird as the mourning dove will have its established pattern of eating and resting, and the bird watcher can have his equipment in a secluded spot and be ready to record when the bird arrives. Silence is a good rule to follow when dealing with any bird.

12 Homing Pigeons in the Fog

> Our soul is escaped as a bird out of the snare of the fowlers: the snare is broken, and we are escaped.   PSALM 124:7

One of our friends who flies his own airplane explains his safety record by saying, "When the homing pigeons don't fly, I don't fly either. Sometimes even they have to wait out the fog."

When fog obscures, there is danger indeed. Old familiar landmarks are blotted out, and there is no easy way to chart a course. The pilot cannot look down and see the winding river, the red roof of the schoolhouse, the church steeple.

His remark about the homing pigeons seemed an exaggeration until one morning in traveling through the South when my husband and I encountered deep marsh fog. Ahead of us in the middle of the road was a beautiful bluish-gray pigeon, which we recognized as akin to those of a young friend whose homing pigeon wins races returning from afar.

Now this bird with the built-in travel mechanism of perfection was inclined to wait out the fog, making no attempt to lift its wings and get into the air. Instead it walked on across the highway toward a bit of grass where the fog seemed a little less. As we moved slowly off the fog-shrouded road to park near the bird, it seemed unafraid of humans or the machine, but rested in front of the bumper.

In the gray fog, the pigeon seemed a ghostly shadow, as it waited quietly for the fog to lift, so that its sense of direction could be followed through the sunlit skies. Almost motionless, the wings were folded back in serene rest, with no agitated moving back and forth impatiently or restlessly.

Looking at the homing pigeon, we thought how different often is our action when fog obscures the path we wish to take. Financial fogs keep us from a desired educational goal, and we fume as we go to work. Later we can see that the particular job really prepared us to accept the other opportunities which arrived for education and greater service.

Often in looking back, we can see how we were not intended to do anything for a little while when the sudden fog swooped down into our lives. If we insisted on action, this sometimes resulted in such failure that work had to be repeated. Wise is the heart which learns how to handle life's fogs through patient waiting as expressed by the homing pigeon.

When fog is treated as a friend, there is less chance

for a gloomy disposition to result from a dark day. Perhaps a foggy morning is the best time for a grandfather to show a child how to put together a difficult jigsaw puzzle. Any child who can learn to play happily on foggy days has one less factor about which to be moody as an adult.

A piece of needlework in the hand can occupy time until sunshine glints from the knitting needle, the crochet hook, or the embroidery thimble. A woodworking bench can provide happy hobby hours until the fog lifts, permitting return to the garden.

Foggy days come to all of us, including God's creatures, the birds. They wait in small clusters on lawns, knowing full well the fog will lift, and they can resume their flight. They do not risk their wings in flying against the fog, but wait to keep them sturdy and strong for later journeys.

If there is deep fog in your life today, surely this is the time to wait and rest, asking God for guidance. Ahead lie the sunlit days for flights into service to community and country, and for fellowship with family and friends.

> *Dear God, forgive us for being afraid of the fogs of life, and especially for our moments of being rebellious at delays.*

*Help us to learn the beautiful intent of
gray days designed to give us time to rest
and gain fresh perspective for the on-
going pattern of our lives. We are grateful
for the example of the birds, who temper
their flight to the weather. Grant us grace
and strength to benefit from our own
foggy days. May we learn the ability to
help others lost in fogs of sadness or
dismaying days of discouragement. Give
us faith to reach out toward the sunshine,
trusting in thee and thy goodness. Amen.*

Suggestions for Bird-watching Enjoyment:

Sometimes a foggy day will produce surprising
visitors at the home feeder. If not, this is a good
time to catch up on the bird research which becomes
an interesting part of bird-watching. One friend
quickly jots down a brief description of a bird the
first time it is sighted, noting such simple items as
"black head, brown body, long bill." Then when she
has time she goes through the bird books until she
discovers a picture or a description which most
nearly matches that of the new bird glimpsed recently. Such informal research adds to the hobby's
pleasures when fog limits the feathery visitors.

13 Cactus Wren Comes Calling

> And God created great whales, and every living creature that moveth, which the waters brought forth abundantly, after their kind, and every winged fowl after his kind: and God saw that it was good. GENESIS 1:21

Not until the third springtime of our bird-watching did cactus wren come calling at our house. Or could it have been that this bird had been there all the time, and we did not recognize its pert appearance?

Our neighbors said they had observed the special little wren in past seasons, but we had not seen it until one memorable morning when sunlight streamed against the feeder and bird bath.

There in a sedate gown with matching hat was a newcomer, paying a call on us. All that seemed to be lacking was a parasol and a purse under one wing to make the call formal and official. We said a happy "Welcome" by throwing out more grain.

Thereafter the wren moved up from the yellow blooming cactus at a regular hour each morning, bringing a new presence into our garden. Many other birds departed for the summer, but this one apparently decided to stay with us, and we had time during hot days and warm twilights to become well acquainted.

The discovery of this wren was the first proof we had that perhaps we were beginning to be able to identify birds. At the start of such watching, they had all looked almost alike. It was hard enough to tell the different kinds of birds apart, much less to learn to identify and call by pet names the individual birds of any type.

Now even the tilt of the tail feathers could help us identify a bird, we realized as we welcomed cactus wren. In fact it was the swishy, upturned tail of the tiny black and white "salt-and-pepper" bird which made us know this newcomer had to be a type of wren.

Through a bird book we confirmed that there was indeed a wren which lived in cactus, and we could see the yellow blossoms on the spiny bush on the hillside below the garden feeder. How glad we were that the bird had taken the initiative in coming to find us, since we were not adept enough to seek it in the brush, even with the aid of binoculars.

Eagerly we came to look for the cactus wren each summer day, aware of this new friend in our feathered flock. Awareness is one of the best gifts which can come into any life. To become aware is a blessing from God, particularly when the awareness extends from birds and animals into the human family.

How often we take it for granted that our friends and family members look as they did several years ago. To become aware that a husband seems preoccupied or falls asleep in his chair earlier than usual may be the first key a wife has that her husband should make an appointment for a physical check-up. Taking a good look at a weary face may be the real clue to starting recovery from insidious illness.

On the other hand, when time is spent looking at the robust cheek of a teen-ager, there may be a fresh awareness that here is an interesting human being who is no longer a child. He is now a young adult, to be treated with mature affection and given responsibility suitable to his increasing powers.

The simple act of becoming aware can lead to greater family happiness and increased fellowship with friends. The faculties of awareness need to be cultivated if such newcomers as the cactus wren are to be welcomed to the garden. The birds speak also of the creator, and can lead to a greater awareness of God and the blessings which come from living in his world of beauty.

Dear God, so many blessings have slipped through our hands because we were not aware of thy bounty while it was there. Some of the friends we loved are gone, and there are empty places in the family circle. May past sorrows not keep us from being aware of the joys of this present day. Let no wandering thoughts of future grandeur keep us from being aware of the riches which are ours at this very moment. Help us to make a start at appreciation of blessings by learning to recognize the birds at our windows. From here may it be an easier step to know of thy great love for us as thy creatures. Keep us aware of happy solutions as well as human problems, trusting thee and thy awareness of us through divine love. Amen.

Suggestions for Bird-watching Enjoyment:

One of the best aids to active bird-watching is a pair of binoculars, which bring distant nests into close vision, as though they were in the garden itself. If we had possessed a good pair of such glasses, probably we would have discovered the cactus wren a year or so earlier. Once we had recognized her in the garden, it was fun to take the binoculars and watch her as she went down into the chaparral. It was an exciting moment of bird-watching when we discovered the bush on which she landed, and then by careful adjusting of the binoculars were able to make out the nest itself. As the hobby of bird-watching grows on the bird lover, the binoculars bring new joys into the home. A pair makes a good joint family birthday present for all ages to enjoy together.

14 Bluebirds for Happiness

How excellent is thy loving-kindness, O God! Therefore the children of men put their trust under the shadow of thy wings.
Psalm 36:7

Of all the sights afforded by the birds on our hilltop, the one I would most like to see repeated time and again concerns the morning when the bluebirds descended for a dance of happiness. Twelve of them stopped by for a drink, arranging themselves around the rim of the large ceramic bowl.

As if by a given signal, each dipped its beak into the cooling water and then brought its head out again, tipping it back to look at the blue sky. Even as we watched the beautiful performance, the silent signal apparently was heard again by the birds, for the action was repeated.

Rhythmically the bluebirds bowed into the water and returned to their original positions, pausing for a moment of enjoyment of the air and the perfume from the nearby rose hedge. The performance contined at leisurely pace for about ten minutes.

Then the bluebirds suddenly left, as quietly and quickly as they had arrived on their beautiful outstretched wings of bright azure shade. This variety had the pinkish red breast, and apparently the feeding had been good, for all were plump and healthy-looking. A more satisfying sight than bluebirds indulging themselves in cool water while they admired their world has seldom come into our vision.

Some of the charm of the moment no doubt lay in the fact that there is traditional happiness in the sight of a bluebird. Many references are made to "bluebirds for happiness" in stories and song, and the bird has become a symbol also on lovely china or needlework patterns.

In my home as a little girl there was a special pitcher with pink roses and a bluebird with outstretched wings. Sometimes this pitcher was brought into use when a child was ill, to pour hot milk over golden brown toast. Happy are the memories of using the little pitcher with the bluebird for happiness.

So it was a great delight to discover the pitcher recently when going through a box of dishes long in storage. When the dust of years was removed and the pitcher immersed in warm sudsy water, it returned to its former clear beauty. The wings of the bluebird seemed as outstretched as ever to encompass happiness, and we placed the little pitcher in the center of the china cabinet.

There we see the bluebird as we walk past on other

errands during the day. Always it reminds us to try to do a little something more each day about cultivating personal happiness. It recalls also the morning when we saw the live bluebirds executing their routine in perfect trust at the bird fountain.

Small wonder that many Bible passages speak of "wings" as a symbol of trust, leading to happiness through an awareness of the loving-kindness of God, the heavenly father. From such trust springs action in behalf of others so that the flight of the bluebirds of happiness may be extended.

This may be something as simple as inviting a neighbor child in for a cookie, or taking time to telephone a newcomer to the church circle. Perhaps it means setting aside an hour for a cup of tea with a friend, neglected in the busy rush of the years.

The bluebirds for happiness are all around us, if we will look for them and let the birds remind us of our current opportunities for fellowship and service. Such shared happiness possesses a blessed wisdom all its own, reminding us that we are indeed children of God, meant to be happy through service in his beautiful world.

*Dear heavenly Father, forgive us for being
unhappy, for we know that a father longs
for happy children. We would measure up
to the highest happiness which thou dost
visualize for us. We are grateful for bodies
useful in this earthly life, but sometimes
these bodies hurt us, and we cannot
manage them as in good health. When this
becomes our problem, send the healing
of happiness into our hearts as well as
our homes, so we may make the greatest
possible strides toward full recovery. May
we keep ourselves well by using our
talents in behalf of others, with our minds
active and our hearts free from self-pity
and resentment. This is a simple prayer,
but what we really want is to be able to
have the bluebirds of happiness with us
as we share together in the milk and
bread of our every-day living. Amen.*

Suggestions for Bird-watching Enjoyment:

Some antics the birds repeat endlessly, but then again
there are rituals which are seen only very occasionally. And it is also true that sometimes the happy

hobby of bird-watching must be almost forgotten when a former hobbyist is confined to a hospital bed without a view. When I visited one such friend recently, she pointed to a picture of a bird on a branch, cut from a magazine cover and affixed with clear tape to the wall nearest her bed. She said that the bird served to remind her of better days, and we talked of the ceramic birds she had brought back from her various travels. These imitations in paper or china can add much daily happiness when placed on a desk or on a windowsill.

15 The Thrasher's Eloquent Song

> The flowers appear on the earth; the time of
> the singing of birds is come . . . SONG OF
> SOLOMON 2:12

When my husband went outside to clip
the fragrant cedar hedge, the birds watched warily
from a distance. They seemed to like to come to the
green "fence" which separated the lawn from the
hill of sage and chaparral, and they had adopted a
proprietary attitude toward the cedar.

From telephone wires nearby they surveyed the
scene of the trimming of the greenery as if to say,
"Did we give you permission to come outside this
morning and take over our hedge?"

Soon they became adjusted to the idea, and began
to sing in tempo to the snipping of the electric
clippers against the hedge. Every once in awhile my
husband would stop the cutting to listen, and he
beckoned me to come outside and join him.

From the sunlit sky there sounded an exquisite
melody, so lovely it seemed truly from another
world. We recalled bits of poetry which have spoken

of the unearthly sounds of beauty which come from the birds. Never before had our ears experienced such a sound of eloquence and joy.

Where could it be coming from? We could identify many of the smaller birds sitting on the wires and poles, and the medium-sized ones which had flown to the big limb overhanging the hilltop. None of them seemed likely suspects.

Surely this sound could not be coming from the big fat bird with the curved beak which we had been watching for days as it dug sharp holes in the lawn and garden, apparently looking for grubs for a meal. The bird used its elaborate curved beak as a hammer and the ground as an anvil, pecking away until some of the holes were so deep they seemed longer than his beak.

This bird seemed meant for utilitarian functions, prepared to defend his size and unusual appearance by the beak, so we had not thought of it as a songbird of any kind. Yet by the process of elimination, this beak seemed to be beaming the music.

We went indoors to consult the bird books, having previously identified our busy visitor with the huge curved beak as a California thrasher. Reading on further, we found reference to the lovely songs of this bird. Taking up the binoculars we brought it closer into range and could see the rise and fall of the large throat.

Loud and clear the thrasher sang on, and the other birds seemed to be quietly listening. We returned to the steps, and the bird did not move from its pole but continued its joyful concert, filling the blue skies with music, an obligato to the breeze in the nearby trees.

When at last the bird had finished, we did not want to stir, much as an audience refrains from clapping after a moving musical experience. Later my husband and I said to each other, "Wrong again; to think we judged that the bird with the beak was not a singer."

Vividly the bird had reminded us of the way we limit ourselves when we make quick and false judgments about others. Judging by appearances always proves disastrous to the one who makes the swift appraisal without taking time to confirm the reasons.

Understanding comes when the individual looks beneath and beyond the appearance, and takes full measure of the stature of those he meets. Perhaps the song of peace itself could be heard a little more clearly if prejudices about size and the unusual could be put aside, and the heart's song identified.

Dear God, forgive us for judging by appearances only. Take from us all negative reactions based on prejudice and intolerance. Grant us wisdom to give the benefit of the doubt to those who seem to us to be different. Indeed grant us the ability to become different, knowing how much our own lives can be improved by contact with that which is out of the ordinary. Help us to learn to listen to the songs of good in the world, and to become quiet enough to let notes of peace slip into our noisy lives. May we learn to extend the boundaries of our understanding by looking past the outer appearance to an inner appreciation of what each of us can offer others in mutual helpfulness. Amen.

Suggestions for Bird-watching Enjoyment:

One way to learn how to identify bird songs is to jot down the date when a new tune is first heard in the garden. Sometimes it is not possible to tell where the song is originating, so make notes of any unusual birds nearby and try to outline the song by syllables. Perhaps there is a new brown bird, or a smaller wren than usual, or a sparrow with different markings. Remember such factors, and then when the song is heard again take another look at the birds present. Eventually the song will be heard when only one bird is there, and you will know for sure where the song originates. Meanwhile the jotted-down song syllables may help when looking through reference books for identification of the singer.

16 Pet Canary Along the Alcan

> The Lord recompense thy work, and a full
> reward be given thee of the Lord God of
> Israel, under whose wings thou art come to
> trust. RUTH 2:12

One summer my husband and I drove the
Alcan Highway to where the roads run out and stop
in beautiful Alaska. We parked beside a small rustic
lodge and went inside for a cup of coffee, and were
instantly greeted by the cheery song of a pet canary
in a golden cage.

The yellow feathers over the tiny throat rose and
fell as if propelled by magic bellows, as the song
carried over the room. A prospector beside the fire-
place smiled in greeting as the pet canary continued
its concert.

A woman appeared behind the counter, tying her
clean apron, and picked up the steaming coffeepot to
pour two big cupfuls. She said we could have our
choice of apple or mince pie, and that the mince-
meat was made from moose she and her husband had
secured on a hunting trip last season.

As we savored the delicious pie and fragrant

coffee, my husband remarked that the canary must offer a lot of good companionship at this comparatively lonely spot along this famous roadway, and the woman replied, "The canary is a member of the firm."

She said that her husband had brought the little pet canary home from one of his jaunts as a trucker, for he knew how homesick she often was for "the outside," the term which those in Alaska give to the states southward.

Immediately the canary had made himself quite at home, and she had been able to teach him some tricks. It was fun to show off the newest tricks when the husband returned from some of his long treks, and if we were interested she would put the canary through the tricks now.

Whereupon the pet canary climbed a little ladder, began to swing from his perch, and then climbed down again to a bar in the golden cage to receive some special seeds from the hands of his owner.

The woman said that with the company of the canary she did not mind so much the long hours of baking the pies at night over a wood stove, after the lodge was closed for the day. Often there were knocks on the door at all hours, from people asking for food, seven days a week.

She and her husband had made a solemn pact that the lodge would not be opened for meals on Sunday, but that they would observe this day for rest, enjoying the scenery themselves and catching up with reading and correspondence.

"Sometimes it is very hard to keep to this rule, but we figure if we can't make it in six days, we can't do it in seven," she said, "and little by little we are making progress."

Often do we remember this simple testimony, accompanied by the obligato from the pet canary, as lovely as a choir anthem. Often a pet will help a human heart over a hard spot in life, enabling one to sing fresh songs of trust.

Undergirded by a cheerful faith, one can attack problems for solution. Many mothers share the experience of baking after the routine of the busy day so there may be fresh cookies for the school lunch box, at a price compatible with a stretched budget.

Many men find it is not easy to earn a living in days of complicated financial patterns, and yet their families must be fed. From those who glean the wheat in the field to those who bake it for family and friends, there is power in learning more of God "under whose wings thou art come to trust."

Such trust receives its recompense, and the faithful heart rejoices in divine companionship, even as the joyful songs of the pet canary add to daily happiness.

*Dear Father, sometimes it is hard to re-
member under whose wings we may come
to trust, as we go our ways alone and
independent of thy help. We thank thee
for the reminders we have from the birds
that thou art the Creator of this universe,
providing for all thy creatures. Even as
the birds find their food in nature or from
human hands, may we always know that
thou art abundantly able to provide for
all our material needs as well as supplying
our inner hopes and aspirations, bringing
dreams to fulfillment. Give us cheerful
hearts as we trust thee for divine recompense to our human labors in behalf of
our loved ones. May our work honor thee
and help our brothers to find greater
happiness. Amen.*

Suggestions for Bird-watching Enjoyment:

If watching the wild birds is not a feasible hobby in
your home, have you investigated the joys of owning
a pet bird, such as a canary or a parakeet? Often
such a pet can provide great therapy for one re-
covering from mental depression or long illness.

Caring for a bird by feeding it regularly and keeping the cage clean is one way to teach children habits of responsibility linked to enjoyment. Such birds provide pleasure also to those in their late years. Recently when visiting in a rest home, I found a very special canary which comes to pay calls on certain friends quite regularly. Its owners bring the lively little bird on their calls, and take it into the rooms for the patients to enjoy. Many were the happy faces up and down the halls where the canary had visited.

17　The Limping Sparrow

> Fear ye not therefore, ye are of more value
> than many sparrows.　MATTHEW 10:31

The first time we saw the limping sparrow,
we couldn't believe our eyes. Here was a bird with
one good leg, and the other so short that the leg
barely hung below the brown feathered wing.

Indeed the bird walked to the seed by limping
from the good leg to the shorter one and almost lying
down on the ground. There it would let the wing
make a huge circle on the dusty earth, by which the
body was propelled forward to the feed.

Steadily the limping sparrow pursued its course
on the ground near our feeder, and we made a mental
note to be sure to see that some extra seed was
scattered to help feed any handicapped birds.

Because of the short leg it was hard for this bird
to maintain proper balance on the rim of the feeder,
even when it managed to fly from the ground. It
seemed to prefer inching along slowly on the ground
beneath the feeder.

The limping sparrow soon became so adept at getting feed in our yard that we ceased to marvel at its unusual ability. Not unless a visitor gave a sharp cry of discovery and called us to the window to see the remarkable bird did we think of its daily struggle.

The other birds came to tolerate the appearance of the sparrow and its clumsy awkward movements. Then one day we discovered the limping sparrow had a friend.

The new sparrow held its head at a strange angle and dipped its little bill to one side as it moved along the ground. Somehow the bill managed to scoop up the feed, whereupon the little bird would straighten up its neck and head and seem to enjoy the meal.

How we longed to be able to help the birds repair their injuries, but they seemed even wilder than the normal wild birds. Perhaps this stemmed in part from their original injuries, and a naturalist friend who observed them felt that both had fallen from the nest when quite young.

"This happens frequently," he told us, "but the birds, if they live and survive the fall, have miraculous powers of adaptation to any handicap caused by an injury."

Watching the two birds preen their feathers in the warm sunlight and pause near the daisies after enjoying the grain, we could not help observing their obvious enjoyment of the day. Their feathers glistened, and the one would rest with his long leg behind it, while the other tipped its head to one side against the grass as a pillow.

Surely, the creator had built into the sparrows the instinctive mechanism for adaptation and survival. Gradually a new concept came into our hearts of what the Bible means when it urges God's children to remember they are of more value than sparrows.

If the birds can adapt to injury, then man with the marvelous discoveries he has made in science and medicine can expect miraculous cures from the injuries of the machine age. The progress may be slow, and one may be clumsy in rehabilitation and the therapy of walking even with new limbs, but the possibility of healing is present within the human body.

Above all, the attitude of fear can be taken out of the discouraged heart, for the admonition comes, "Fear not." The sparrows walked fearlessly among their kind, accepting the grain provided, and enjoying the day's blessing. With fear removed, the process of healing can take place not only physically, but for the bruised heart and weary mind.

*Father, often we are fearful not only for
ourselves but for those we love. We see
them involved in fast-driven machines, or
tempted by drugs and new attitudes of
permissiveness. Help us not to take counsel of our fears, but to trust in thee, the
Creator, who gives us the healing of faith,
compassion, and love. If we have been
injured, grant us the maximum power of
recovery within our strength and means.
If we must learn to live with certain limi-
tations, grant the patience necessary.
Above all, spare us from self-pity, the
most crippling of all emotions, and grant
to our hearts the ability to leap over ob-
stacles because we trust in thy care and
the value thou dost place on each of us.
Amen.*

Suggestions for Bird-watching Enjoyment:

One way to help the birds to strength is by providing
extra fuel through suet or meat fats. A friend pokes
a hole through a piece of suet, runs string through
the hole, and ties the treat to her favorite tree, where
the birds come to "refuel." We save all the fats from

roasts and cool this in our "bird pan," a covered coffee can kept in the refrigerator. When cold we spread the grease on bits of breadcrust and take them outside for a bird feast. Another family puts all its grease drippings in a baking pan, adds old bread, some sugar, and a little water, and slips this into the oven simultaneously with a gingerbread loaf. The "bird pudding" is cut into strips or squares and the birds love it as much as family and friends enjoy the spicy cake.

18 A Laughing Mockingbird

> I will abide in thy tabernacle for ever:
> I will trust in the covert of thy wings. Selah.
> PSALM 61:4

The word "selah" occurring at the end of many psalms has something of the call of the wild birds in it. Often as they visit together in the tree branches, the sound comes echoing, "Selah, selah, selah."

As explained in Bible literature this word was used by the congregation in concluding the psalms which had been read by the leaders. All voices joined together in praise through the use of the simple word "selah."

It has a rhythm to it which the birds can easily use in making up their daily songs. And it is an easy phrase for the birds which "mock" to call back and forth to one another. Indeed we have heard two mockers on our hilltop seeming to shout "selah" back and forth, just for the sound of their own music and to talk to each other.

Mockers will try anything, including the imitating

of cats, so that in some parts of the country they are known as "catbirds." We ourselves have the "laughing mocking bird," which likes nothing better than to sit on the topmost limb of the biggest tree, look over the world, and laugh its head off at the rest of us.

The first time we heard the sound we thought there must indeed be a person outside the window, laughing endlessly at some secret joke. Could it be a lost child, laughing because he was tired of crying?

I pulled back curtains, and looked out of various windows, but could find no trace of a human figure. Still the laughter continued, more loudly than ever, once I had closed the drapes again and tried to get back to the typewriter.

A shadow flew past the window, and I cautiously got out of the chair to see where the shadow had landed. It belonged to the largest mocker I had ever seen. This time the mockingbird decided the moment had come for introductions.

To my call "Oh, there you are," the mocker replied with a crescendo of laughter, as much as to say, "I sure fooled you for awhile, didn't I?"

Now the laughing mocker is our clown jester of the garden. When I get too involved with problems, whether they involve a sentence or a recipe, I go in search of the laughing mocker.

In return for a bread crust, for which it will fight off the bluejays, the mocker will reward us with laughter. Indeed it is almost impossible to keep from laughing at the antics of the bird as it feuds with the large jay over foodstuffs. The jay may give a shrill call of disgust and then chatter in dismay, but the mocker just keeps on laughing.

Sometimes we try to tempt the mocker to put on a laughing concert for friends, but he is a sly one with his own brand of wit, and he will not laugh on cue. Yet whenever he does decide to "sing" he includes some giggles and a few good guffaws.

Then we stop working and laugh with him, stepping to the window just to try the exercise of deep laughter. This elemental sound is highly recommended by doctors, particularly those who deal with emotional problems.

They say there is healing in the therapeutic value of laughter, and we think our mocker must have been listening in through some window when laughter was prescribed as an antidote for depression.

Certainly the laughing mockingbird keeps busy just laughing his songs throughout the garden. Continually he is a pleasure to have around, for he reminds us to laugh at ourselves and not think life's dreary problems too hard for solution.

Dear Father, we are so grateful for the joys of laughter, often heard in the first cooing sounds of the babies in our homes. Forgive us for forgetting to laugh as we grow older. Help us to remember that a merry heart truly doeth good like a medicine, and that sometimes when we cannot do anything else to help another, we can at least laugh at the remembrance of happy days in the past. Give us lighter hearts for the carrying of each day's burden, and may we never be too serious to stop for a moment's respite in laughing relaxation. We ask for smiles to share with others, and the ability to relax with laughter at the end of the long day, keeping always the blessing of cheerful hearts. Amen.

Suggestions for Bird-watching Enjoyment:

That no two seasons will ever be quite alike is an important fact for any bird watcher to learn early. One season may bring the mockingbird which laughs, but by another year he may move on to other feeding grounds. Therefore it is of interest to keep a simple notebook in which such facts can be jotted down. A friend notes by weeks the time when certain birds arrive, and then when she realizes they are gone again, she tries to remember the last day she saw them and writes down that date. Then another year she knows when to expect such birds and how long they may linger. By this simple technique she has become her own "expert" and a source of delightful information for her friends, who call her for confirmation about the possible arrival of a certain bird.

19 Wise Young Owls

But unto you that fear my name shall the Sun of righteousness arise with healing in his wings. MALACHI 4:2

Bird-watching by night can be one of the most thrilling adventures for family enjoyment. We discovered it quite by accident when we came upon a family of owls nesting in the soft cliffs of a canyon near our home.

As we were driving our car slowly one moonlit night, the big wingspan of an owl flashed across our windshield, moving from the side of the canyon road up to the hillside, where the bird stopped suddenly.

Quietly we drove up the canyon to where we might turn around and park the car on a wide spot of the road, and watch to see if the owl came back. The bird appeared very soon, flying across in search of more food to take back to the unseen nest.

Satisfied that the owl family lived nearby, we made plans to return at some later date to try to fathom more of the owl habits. This is how we happened to discover the wise young owls, who taught us much.

We learned that if we parked the car, and each looked out of the window on our side, we could get a good view of the holes in the cliff. From the largest of these, the owl we soon called "Father Owl" would appear, often followed by "Mother Owl."

After a few nights of watching, we saw the fuzzy head of a young owl appear at the hole to the cliff nest. No longer was it necessary for the parent owls to go inside to feed, as the babies had been trained to come to the entry way for their food.

We were privileged to be watching on the historic night when the most adventuresome of the tiny owlets came out to try to learn to fly. Such coaxing it took to get the owl to move even a little way from the nest! We held our breath as it seemed the little owl was about to fall, but by a clumsy maneuvering of both wings and legs, the owl caught its balance on the cliff.

Then came piteous cries for help as the frightened owl tried to decide whether to go up or to go down. Obviously it could not remain so perilously perched for much longer, and the decision evidently was reached to go on as the father and mother were calling directions.

With a whoosh of the wings, the little owl made

it to the nearest twig, sitting there with puffed out chest, more in pride than in fear. The parent owls hovered nearby, giving stacatto exclamations, which we hoped were in praise of their wise, courageous owlet.

He had obeyed his parents in coming out further from the nest, and not retreating or staying in limbo. Now he could look back to the spot from which he had come. Indeed he could fly on back and tell the other little owl in the nest what it was like out in the big wide world, beneath the stars.

We remembered the eyes blinking against the car lights as we started thoughtfully homeward. Happily we had shared the thrill of the wise young owl, who learned the joys of taking his "first steps" in flight.

Often do I think of the wise young owl as I look at a lovely owl figurine on my writing desk. This one is made of pink luminous glass with blue jeweled eyes, and is the gift of a friend, who offered it as an omen of wisdom.

Like the memory of the young owl flying, it speaks of the wisdom of trying to take the first step toward reaching a goal, even as the wise young owl triumphed over its fear of the unknown.

Dear God, grant us wisdom and give us strength for meeting the demands of each day. Let us remember always that the most difficult problem may be broken down into easy steps if we ask for guidance in reaching decisions as to what to do first. When we reach the point of indecision as to what to do next, help us to take the way forward and not turn back from achievement. When we have tested our wings on the smaller tasks of life, give us greater goals to achieve, that we may know the constant joy of growth. Keep us from trusting our own wisdom, but may we always defer to thee and thy greater wisdom as to what is best for our lives. Amen.

Suggestions for Bird-watching Enjoyment:

Many legends and traditions spring up about birds, and certain words attach to certain birds as if they were feathers. Thus it is that everyone thinks of "wise owls." The time comes in the hobby of bird-watching when the individual discovers that, without realizing it, he has acquired quite a bit of wisdom about the birds. And one family's knowledge is different perhaps from that of the neighbors. One bird watcher automatically seems to gravitate toward another bird watcher, and soon they are exchanging notes. Let one of these acquaintances tell you the name of an unfamiliar bird, and you will have made a new friend as well as identified the bird friend. Fellow bird lovers are almost always generous people, willing to share and receive knowledge.

20 Wild Geese Flying Homeward

> He shall cover thee with his feathers, and under his wings shalt thou trust: his truth shall be thy shield and buckler. PSALM 91:4

An old gardener friend digging near the birdbath said to me, "You will never see anything lovelier in this life than the sight of the wild geese flying homeward."

He leaned on his spade and added, "When I was a boy on the farm, the sound of the wild geese honking as they went over our house made me want to go out and see the world, so I became a sailor."

Together we paused and thought about the places he had seen in his many years of travel on the water before he retired to the land. Now he seemed to enjoy gardening chores in supplementing his income.

"Do you want to know what the wild geese mean to me now?" he said shyly. "They show me the way home now that I am an old man."

Although he was young in appearance, we both knew he was nearing the head of the procession of the years. Happy are all those who feel that they are arrayed in life's formation, following a sure leader, as do the wild geese in the autumn sky.

As the wild geese fly overhead, they stream in two columns behind one uniform leader, who has been selected at the beginning of the race. He keeps unerringly to the uncharted path through the skies, possessed of wisdom and stamina.

When the birds go down for water or food in some isolated spot large enough to shelter them, it is this leader who signals when they must take off again.

There is something so reassuring in the sight of the wild geese flying homeward, as if they were guided by unseen hands and voices which the human ear cannot discern at present.

The family which watches together as the wild geese fly overhead cannot help feeling a sense of awe and wonder at this example of a trusted leader and his willing followers.

Often mankind feels alone and lost in making the all-encompassing journey through life toward eternity. Yet it is not necessary to make this trek without a leader, and without voices of guidance.

The Bible gives its counsel of hope and faith to counteract distrust and fear. It speaks of the provisions God has made for his creatures and children.

There are many definite promises, and often these use the symbolism of the birds. Indeed in the Psalms the figure of God himself is clothed in the picture we see in the birds as they fly homeward.

The Psalms promise that mankind may safely trust under the "wings of God," and that the maker will "cover thee with his feathers."

Soft but strong are the feathers of God as touched by the soul of seeking man. They enable each heart to take its proper place in the long procession heading to the eternal homeland.

For this journey homeward, the truth of God is available to all who seek, asking in prayer for guidance and strength for each new day.

Father, we thank thee for the wonderful beauty of the wild geese flying homeward. We ask thee to give us the sure and certain knowledge that we may have thy care each day as we make our own journeys toward thy eternal home. Keep us ever mindful of the beauties of this earth in which we learn our lessons of faith and trust, discarding fear and discouragement as unnecessary feathers no longer needed along the skyway which leads to thee. Keep us clean and fit for the flight, with eyes and hearts which recognize and

*know our leader. Let our faith be such
that others may know we follow thee and
may want to join the long procession
which leads to thy eternal home. Amen.*

Suggestions for Bird-watching Enjoyment:

Bird-watching is a hobby to "grow into" without
tension or strain—by relaxing and enjoying what has
been placed in God's world for the enjoyment of all
his children. From watching alone in an easy chair
by the window, it is a natural step outdoors to the
garden. Some families find pleasure in going with
friends on bird walks or "counts," and perhaps join-
ing organizations dedicated to preservation of wild
life. Certainly at such a moment as when the wild
geese are flying homeward, the heart lifts automatically, as birds flying in perfect formation follow
some hidden rhythm, ageless as time. Gratitude for
such priceless experiences can be expressed in con-
servation of the good earth and protection of the
beautiful birds, as they sing their lovely songs of
praise and thanksgiving.